CASTLES

CONTENTS

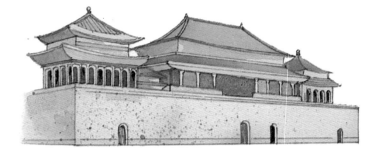

WHY BUILD A CASTLE?

The first houses ever built provided protection from the weather and wild animals. Unfortunately, some houses were also targets for robbers and invaders. To protect themselves and their homes, people built walls around their houses. These were the first castles.

Ancient Hill Fort
Hill forts, built in northern Europe about 3,000 years ago, had walls made of earth. The maze at the entrance was designed to confuse enemies.

Motte-and-Bailey Castle
Sometimes a large ditch, called a **moat**, was dug around the house and filled with water. The extra soil from the moat was piled into a small hill called a **motte.** Then a fence was built around the motte. The fenced-in area was known as the **bailey.**

Stone Castle
About 900 years ago, the first stone castles were built. Stone castles were safer than wood castles because stone does not burn. The **keep**, part of the main tower, was the safest place in the castle.

A STONE CASTLE

Stone castles were designed so that the people inside would be safe and secure. Enemies approaching from any side could be spotted from round towers. The round towers were sturdy and very difficult to knock down.

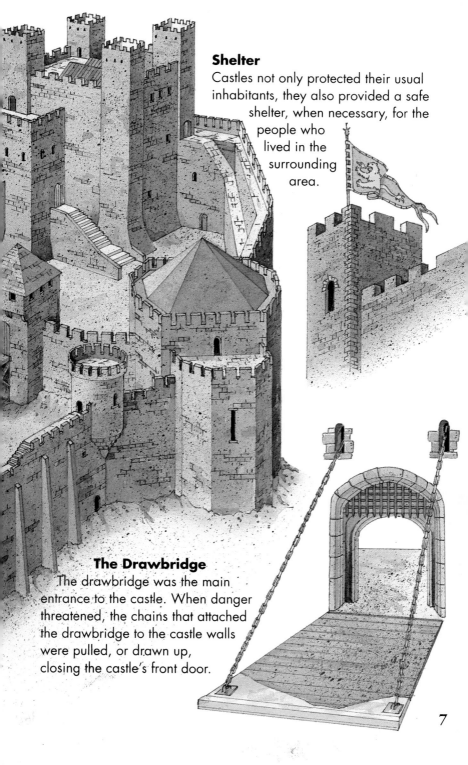

Shelter

Castles not only protected their usual inhabitants, they also provided a safe shelter, when necessary, for the people who lived in the surrounding area.

The Drawbridge

The drawbridge was the main entrance to the castle. When danger threatened, the chains that attached the drawbridge to the castle walls were pulled, or drawn up, closing the castle's front door.

A DAY IN A CASTLE

Life at the castle was always busy and exciting. Most of the time, it was a place where people lived and worked peacefully, rather than a battleground.

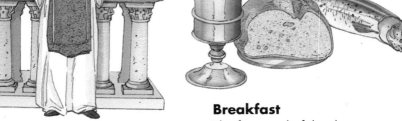

Religion
The day often began with prayers in the castle chapel.

Breakfast
The first meal of the day was usually bread and water. Sometimes, meat and fish were also served. Because there was no refrigeration, cooks preserved food by drying, smoking, or salting it. Food was stored in the keep, where it was cool and dark.

Lessons
Children were taught to read and write by monks or priests. Girls also learned to sew, and boys practiced archery and other skills. After lessons, girls and boys played games such as **stoolball**.

Hunting

Trained hawks and falcons were used to hunt rabbits, birds, and other small game animals. Hounds, or hunting dogs, were trained to hunt larger animals, such as wild boar and deer. People also fished for eel and pike, which were favorite meals.

Dinner

Members of the household would eat meat and fish and drink wine in the great hall of the castle. They sat at long **banquet** tables and were often entertained between courses by minstrels, jugglers, and other performers. On special occasions, as many as forty courses might be served!

Bedtime

The lord and lady slept in the **solar,** the biggest and warmest bedroom in the castle. Most of the other residents slept in the great hall, where the fire would burn all night for warmth.

ATTACKING A CASTLE

An enemy army's best plan of attack was to take the castle occupants by surprise. Invaders tried to **scale,** or climb over, the walls under cover of darkness. If that didn't work, they would try to break through the castle's outer walls. With the help of catapults, enemies hurled boulders at and over castle walls. The largest catapult was the **trebuchet**. It could launch rocks more than 300 feet.

Crossbows and Arrows
Archers with crossbows fired from behind a wooden screen called a **mantlet.**

If the army still had not gained entry to the castle, they might lay **siege**. During a seige, the outside army prevented anyone or anything from going into or coming out of the castle. A siege could last for many months. Without supplies of fresh food and water, the castle occupants would eventually surrender or starve.

Catapult

DEFENDING A CASTLE

Castle dwellers kept plenty of food and drink stored away in case of a siege. When they sighted the enemy, they raised the drawbridge and for extra protection, lowered a strong iron gate called a **portcullis**. Archers in the castle fired arrows through window slits, called **arrow loops**, in the castle walls. The small size and narrow shape of these openings gave archers a good view of the enemy and made it difficult for the enemy's arrows to hit them.

Cauldron
A large pot was used to pour boiling liquids on the enemy below.

Parts of the battlements stuck out over the ground below, so heavy stones could be dropped down on the enemy. These were known as **murder holes**.

Archery
Archers used two types of bow: the longbow and the crossbow. The longbow was made from springy yew wood and fired hard ash-wood arrows with steel tips. A strong arm was needed to use a longbow. Crossbows were easier to shoot. They fired shorter arrows that were also very deadly.

KNIGHTS

Knights were soldiers and commanders in a castle's army. They rode strong, powerful horses into battle and wore heavy, protective armor.

Helmet
A movable visor helped to protect the knight's face.

Sword
A pointed sword was good for thrusting through gaps in armor.

Battleaxe
This weapon was especially useful on horseback.

Mace
Ridges on the head of the mace concentrated the force of the blow.

Shield
Every knight was identified by the symbol on his shield. All of the symbols were part of a special system called **heraldry.** When a knight died, his symbol was passed on to his eldest son.

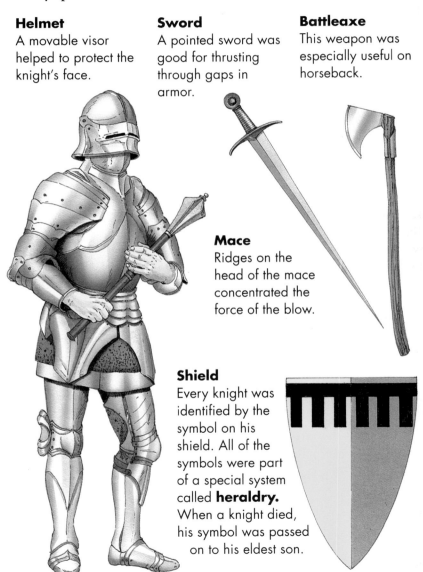

DOORS AND WINDOWS

The design of the doors and windows of a castle were important. They had to be easy to close and secure if the castle was under attack.

Parapets
Some castles had wooden planks, called **parapets**, that stuck out from the exterior walls.

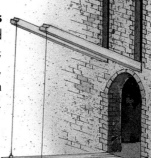

Arrow Loops
These windows were too narrow for intruders to climb through.

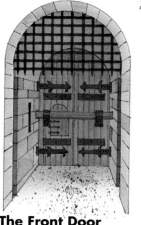

Machicolations
Turrets or platforms called **machicolations** jutted out from the walls.

The Front Door
A solid wood door and an iron gate protected the main entrance.

Great Hall Window
Glass was expensive. Only the wealthy might have a window like this in the main or great hall.

KNIGHTS IN PEACETIME

Boys from wealthy families could train to become knights. It could take ten years of hard work and study. These boys learned by serving knights, first as **pages**, then as **squires**. Their duties included cleaning knights' heavy armor. In return, the knights taught their squires how to behave as leaders and fight with different weapons.

Knights fought in a type of tournament called a **joust**. In a joust, two knights charged at each other with long wooden poles called lances. For safety, the two knights were separated by a low wooden fence, called a tilt. If one knight was knocked off his horse, the other would dismount and the fight would continue on the ground.

Food was kept in
storehouses and in the
castle keep. Horses lived
in the stable. Chickens
and other livestock
provided the occupants
with fresh eggs and meat.

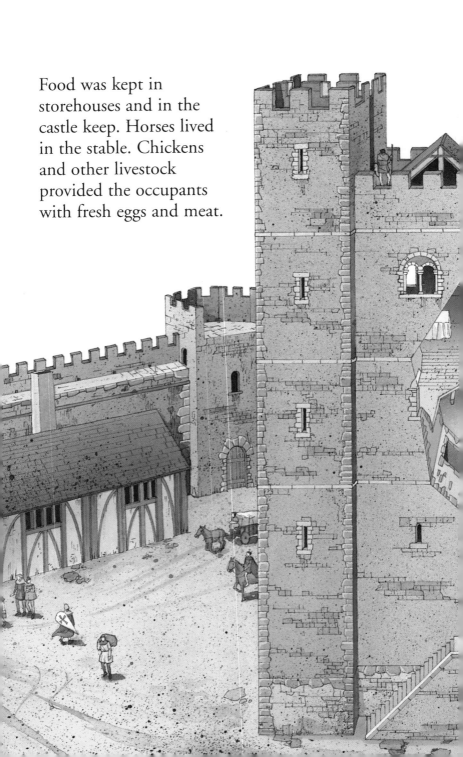

LIFE AT A MEDIEVAL CASTLE

Many castles were built during the Middle Ages or Medieval times, about nine hundred years ago. In those days, horses and carts were the main means of transportation. Oxen were used to pull heavy carts and plough the fields outside the castle walls. People brought goods into the castle through the **gatehouse**.

Many castles had stone toilets that were built into the outer walls. Inside the castle walls were other buildings. Most of them were made of wood.

A dependable water source was vital to castle life. Many castles were built over underground springs, ensuring that castle dwellers would have fresh drinking water even during a seige. Underground springs were also safe from enemies' attempts to poison the water. Some castles had secret tunnels that could be used to escape during a seige.

Castles had little furniture. Reeds and herbs were often used to cover bare floors. Woven tapestries were hung on walls to help keep the castle warm.

Captured enemies and dangerous criminals were locked up in the dungeon, the castle's prison. Prisoners sometimes carved pictures on the stone walls to pass the time. Especially dangerous prisoners might be chained to the walls for many years.

WHO'S WHO IN THE CASTLE

Many people lived and worked in a castle. It was often possible to tell the kind of work people did by noticing what they wore or what they carried.

Soldier
The castle's defender, a soldier carried weapons such as bows, arrows, and swords.

Jester
Recognized by his colorful costume with bells on his hat, a jester's job was to keep the nobles amused.

Minstrel
A minstrel sang and played musical instruments to entertain the household.

Serf
A serf was a manual laborer who worked in the fields and helped build and repair the castle.

Bowman
Like the soldier, a bowman helped protect the castle.

Maintaining a castle required a lot of people and a lot of money. Money was collected in the form of taxes or rents to pay for the upkeep of the castle.

Constable

The constable made sure that everything in the castle ran smoothly. He had to be aware of strangers visiting the castle, in case the strangers were spies.

Marshall

The marshall organized the accommodations, especially when guests came to visit and stay.

Butler

Planning and serving meals was the butler's main responsibility.

Steward

The steward rode all over the surrounding lands, seeing that the estate was in order.

BUILDING CASTLES

Building a castle took many years. All the work was done by hand. People with specialized skills were hired to oversee and carry out the construction. More than a thousand laborers might be working on the castle at any given time.

Master Mason

The master mason was the medieval architect. He drew up the plans for the castle to meet the lord's specifications.

Scaffolding

As the castle walls rose, wooden scaffolding was erected so builders could work higher and higher up the walls. Scaffolding was made of poles bound together with rope. Wooden platforms were laid on top. Workers climbed ladders to reach these platforms.

Stonemason

The stonemason carefully shaped large and small blocks of stone to fit together.

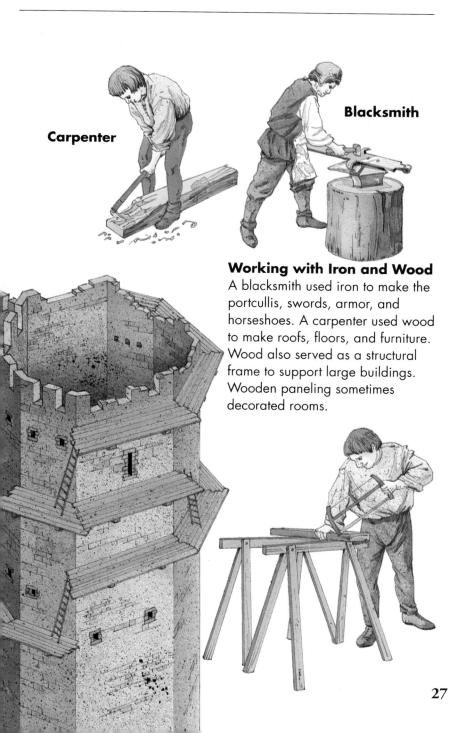

Carpenter

Blacksmith

Working with Iron and Wood
A blacksmith used iron to make the portcullis, swords, armor, and horseshoes. A carpenter used wood to make roofs, floors, and furniture. Wood also served as a structural frame to support large buildings. Wooden paneling sometimes decorated rooms.

CASTLES TODAY

Some castles have been preserved, but many of the earliest castles decayed and now lie in ruins. The ruins of ancient castles do not have roofs because the wood rotted away, leaving only the stonework behind.

Chillon on Lake Geneva

This castle in Switzerland is more than 1,000 years old. The whole castle was once used as a prison.

Palaces

Fancy castles, built for comfort and to display wealth, are called palaces. Many palaces have huge gardens.

Windsor Castle

Windsor Castle is one of the homes of the British royal family. In 1993, a fire swept through part of the castle, causing major damage.

Edinburgh Castle

The remains of a castle on this site in Scotland can be traced back to A.D. 600. Edinburgh Castle was built on a steep-sided rock, which stands almost 400 feet above the surrounding ground. This rock is the remains of an ancient volcano. The castle overlooks the city of Edinburgh, which grew under the protection of the castle. The English captured this site several times during the Middle Ages. It was later taken back by the Scots.

CASTLES AROUND THE WORLD

Many types of castles have been built in countries around the world. Although most castles were built to defend an area and its inhabitants, every castle was different. Sometimes castles had to be built in odd shapes to fit into certain areas. Some were also built to protect communications routes, such as roads and rivers. Castles in certain countries had distinctive features. Many French castles, for example, had pointed roofs on their turrets.

Krak des Chevaliers

This 12th century castle was built in Syria, in the Middle East. Sloping mounds of soil around the base made it difficult for attackers to tunnel underneath. This castle still stands, although it has been damaged by earthquakes.

Ruins of Zimbabwe

In Zimbabwe, Africa, the ruins of an ancient walled city, built in the 9th century, still stand. Treasure, weapons, and gold objects have been found in these ruins.

The Tower of London

This fortress, built in 1087 in London, England, by William the Conqueror, is now home to the British crown jewels. It is sometimes called "The White Tower" because the keep's walls were painted white to look more impressive from a distance.

Rheinfels

One of the strongest castles ever built, Rheinfels stands on a steep rock above the Rhine River in Germany. Constructed in the 13th century, it has never been conquered.

City of Azulchi

The fortress city of Azulchi was built in the 16th century by the warlords of Japan. The city's castle had a central tower seven stories high. The walls were decorated with paintings and beautiful carvings.

PALACES

Since castles were built to protect people, they were safe, but not especially comfortable. Palaces, however, were luxurious, comfortable, and ornate. They were built to display the wealth and importance of their owners.

Hampton Court

Cardinal Wolsey built this palace in the 16th century for King Henry VIII. Located just outside London, Hampton Court has been carefully restored and is open to visitors. The tall hedges in the garden form a challenging maze.

The Alhambra

This "Red Fortress" was built by the Moors in Granada, Spain, in the 14th century. The Alhambra is made of pink bricks and is surrounded by pools of water and beautifully landscaped, shady courtyards.

The Forbidden City

Built in the 13th century in Beijing, China, the "Forbidden City" is surrounded by walls and large gates. Emperors lived in the Forbidden City with their families and many servants. Everyone else was forbidden to enter its walls.

Chichen-itza

The city of Chichen-itza, in Mexico's Yucatan province, was the center of the Mayan empire. A temple built like a pyramid is shown here. There are many other buildings in the city, dating back to A.D. 500. These include a courtyard with many columns and an observatory tower, built to study the stars and planets.

Schönbrunn

This magnificent palace, built near Vienna, Austria, was the home of the Austrian emperors. It is nearly 300 years old and has more than 1,400 rooms, including a theater and a hall of mirrors.

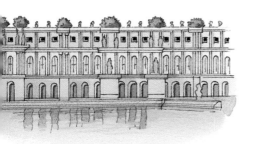

Versailles

This beautiful palace, near Paris, France, was originally built by King Louis XIII. His extravagant son, Louis XIV, known as the "Sun King," spent a fortune making the palace and gardens bigger and even more beautiful.

LANDMARK BUILDINGS

Castles are not the only distinctive buildings in which people have lived, worked, and worshiped throughout history. A variety of structures, such as pyramids, columns, arches, and domes, originated in different areas of the world. These architectural features create a legacy of landmarks, from different places and times, for us to visit.

1. Pyramid
Built in Egypt about 5,000 years ago, pyramids were the tombs of kings.

2. Stonehenge
Stone columns were erected in England about 4,000 years ago. No one knows why or for whom.

3. Greek column
Greeks first used columns to support roofs about 2,500 years ago.

4. Roman arch
Romans first used arches to support buildings about 2,000 years ago.

5. Hindu *stupa*
Buddhists built these gold mounds in Asia 1,500 years ago.

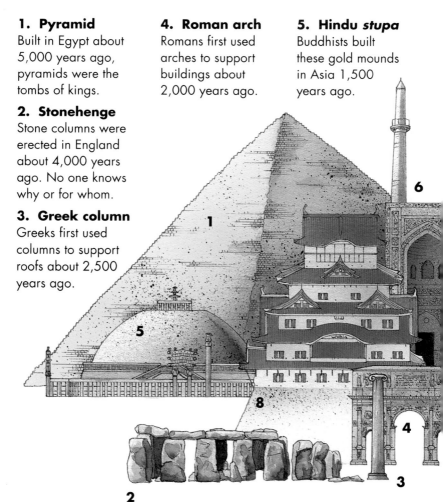

6. Mosque
First built in the Middle East about 1,450 years ago, mosques are houses of worship.

7. Aztec temple
These temples were built by the Aztec civilization in South America, about 750 years ago.

8. Japanese castle
About 400 years ago, Japanese nobles built castles called *daimyos*.

9. Taj Mahal
Built in India about 300 years ago, the Taj Mahal was a tomb for a much-loved Indian empress.

10. Russian cathedral
Built in Russia about 300 years ago, the cathedral's domes were specially shaped so snow would slide off them.

11. Empire State Building
Erected in 1931 in New York City, this skyscraper has 102 stories and is 1,454 feet tall.

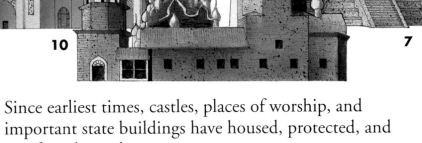

Since earliest times, castles, places of worship, and important state buildings have housed, protected, and comforted people.

AMAZING CASTLE FACTS

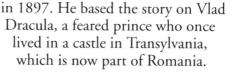

- **Windows** Most castle windows were covered with oiled linen or animal skins, to protect against drafts.

- **Pigeons** Many castles kept pigeons — not as messengers, but for food.

- **The oldest castle** The oldest castle in the world was built in the Middle East in A.D.100. It stood twenty stories high.

- **Beijing Palace** Moats around the Imperial Palace in Beijing, China, measure 148 feet wide — wider than many rivers.

- **A castle in two parts** Part of the castle of Burg Wildenstein was perched on a hilltop overlooking the Danube River in Germany. The other part of the castle was on a nearby hill. A tall tower with walkways linked them together.

- **Castle of horror** The Irish writer Bram Stoker wrote *Dracula* in 1897. He based the story on Vlad Dracula, a feared prince who once lived in a castle in Transylvania, which is now part of Romania.

- **Monster hunting** The ruins of Urquhart Castle overlook Loch Ness, a lake in Scotland. The site of the ruins is supposedly one of the best places to see the famous monster that is rumored to live in the lake.

GLOSSARY

Arrow loops Narrow holes in the castle walls through which archers shot arrows.

Bailey The fenced area of land, around a motte, where people lived and worked.

Banquet An elaborate meal or feast with many different courses.

Gatehouse An entry point to the castle that was often heavily guarded.

Heraldry A medieval system for classifying knights using symbols.

Joust A type of fight between two knights, mainly on horseback.

Keep A castle's central tower and strongest defense point. It was also used for food storage.

Machicolation Part of a battlement that stuck out over the castle walls. This structure might have holes in the floor, so that heavy boulders and hot liquids could be dropped onto attackers.

Mantlet A wooden screen used to protect archers who were firing at a castle.

Moat A deep ditch, usually filled with water, surrounding a castle.

Motte A large hill made with soil dug from around a castle.

Murder hole An opening in the battlement through which heavy objects were dropped.

Page A boy in the first stage of training to be a knight.

Parapet A wall or plank projecting outward from the edge of a platform.

Portcullis A strong grating, usually made of iron, that could be lowered to protect the front door of a castle.

Scale To climb up or over.

Siege A military blockade in which an attacking army prevents food, water, and supplies from entering a castle, forcing the occupants to surrender or starve.

Solar The biggest, warmest, and best-lit bedroom in the castle, used by the lord and lady.

Squire A young man in the second stage of training for knighthood.

Stoolball A ball game, similar to baseball, played by children during the Middle Ages.

Trebuchet French for "bouncer," a large catapult that fired boulders at the castle walls.

INDEX *(Entries in **bold** refer to an illustration)*